2ND EDITION
BIG TV WORKBOOK

Pearson Education Limited
KAO Two
KAO Park
Harlow
Essex CM17 9NA
England
and Associated Companies throughout the world.

www.English.com/BigEnglish2

First published 2017

ISBN: 978-1-292-20362-1

Set in Heinemann Roman

Printed in Italy by L.E.G.O. S.p.A.

Acknowledgements
The publisher would like to thank the following for their kind permission to reproduce their photographs:

(Key: b-bottom; c-centre; l-left; r-right; t-top)
123RF.com: 3lt (plastic), Akz 12t, 14tl, Wisnu Ali 15t (talent show), Galyna Andrushko 37tc, Artisticco 13tr, Artisticco LLC 7t (basketball), 7t (tennis), 15t (bus), 15t (chess), Bloomua 26 (tablet), Blueringmedia 23 (Ryan), Louilia Bolchakova 27b, Brgfx 23 (Susie), Kanate Chainapong 35tl (USA), Cheskyw 3lt (3D printer), Dolgachov 22t, 26b, ekzardho 27t (tablet), Elena Elisseeva 8/5, Epicstockmedia 36/1, Eraxion 28/4, Eros Erika 5bl, experimental 19tr, Surgey Furtaev 8/8, Vladimir Galkin 5br, Gelpi 7cl, 11cl, 19cr, 23bl, 35cl, 39cr, Gjohnstonphoto 29tl, Goodluz 8/7, Vadim Guzhva 14cr, Homydesign 36/8, ildogesto 26 (microphone), Ilgogesto 26 (camera), 26 (speakers), Ben Jeayes 33tr, juliatim 3lt (headset), Nuttaphong Kanchanachaya 35tl (Egypt), Dzmitry Kliapitski 38, Pavel Konovalov 2ltr, Daria Kovtun 35tr (avocados), Andrei Krauchuk 13tc, 23 (Katie), Dejan Krsmanovic 10t, Sergey Lavrentev 13tl, limages 23 (Zoe), Alejandro Lozano Campana 35tl (Mexico), lucadp 30b, Luckybusiness 24/2, Macrovector 26 (touchscreen), Mangostar 16b, mezzotint123rf 5tc, MichaelJun 8/4, Mihtiander 9tc, Fernando Gregory Milan 2ltr, Claudia Mora 35tr (ice cream), moremarinka 3lt (clean water), mrdoomits 18t, Teguh Mujiono 15t (swimming), Neyro2008 11 (Ben), 11 (Erica), 11 (Grant), 11 (Jeannie), 11 (Man), 11 (Maria), Nitr 33cr, Win Nondakowit 3lt (make bags), Odua Images 13b, 27cl, 35cr, Pat Olson 25l, Oxygen64 15t (books), Songsak Paname 34, Photobac 37tr, Pixelery 25b, Ganna Poltoratska 30t, Andriy Popov 29b, Maxim Popov 15t (basketball), Redrockerz 15t (sports competition), Robuart 27t (digital camera), Scott Sanders 36/2, David Schneider 28/7, Shariffc 4b, Tatiana Shepeleva 24/8, Dmitriy Shironosov 8/1, 10b, Michael Simons 24/4, Slena 8/2, studioworkstock 3lt (make cars), Tatiana Suslova 7b, Mikhail Terskov 22b, Tomaccojc 15b, Vinga 14tc, Waeruswan Waesemae 35tl (Italy), Waeruswan Waeseman 35tl (the Netherlands), Wavebreak Media Ltd 32, Pauliene Wessel 33cl, Ximagination 5tl, Nataliya Yakoleva 26 (avatar), Cathy Yeulet 8/6, 14c, Yganko 35tr (tulips), yupiramos 24/3, Zhukovviad 5bc, Юлия Саенкова 23 (Zander); **Pearson Education Ltd:** Amit John 35tr (cotton), Arvind Singh Negi / Red Reef Design Studio. Pearson India Education Services Pvt. Ltd 15t (hospital), 15t (school), Pearson Education Ltd 15t (race), Pradip Kumar Bhowal. Pearson India Education Services Pvt. Ltd 39tr, Shivani Anshuk. Pearson India Education Services Pvt. Ltd 7t (skiing), Anirban Sarkar 39tl, Ian Wedgewood 24/7; **Shutterstock.com:** 17cr, Akemaster 5tr, Amenic181 2ltl, Nuno Andre 3lt (robotic arm), Aristicoo 7t (soccer), 7t (swimming), ArtmannWitte 36/3, AvDe 37tl, B Calkins. 14tr, Blend Images 8/3, Bloomua 24/1, Diego Cervo 9tl, Civdis 36/4, Donna Ellen Coleman 13cl, 23br, 39cl, Eurobanks 7cr, 15cr, FashionStock.com 6, Ferenc Szelepscseny 17bl, Iakov Filimonov 17cl, Georgejmclittle 17br, Germanskydive 36/5, Nicole Gordine 3lt (print toys), Granata68 9tr, Johann Heigason 28/3, Hin255 17tr, Hurst Photo 14b, Hxdbzxy 17tl, Ilolab 33tl, Ammit Jack 36/7, Jane Kelly 27t (smartphone), Robyn Mackenzie 29tr, Maniola 29tc, Skoropadska Maruna 28/2, Jiratthitikain Maurice 28/5, Monkey Business Images 9b, 14cl, 16t, Ociacia 3lt (robot), Anna Om 11cr, 19cl, 3lbr, OPOLJA 24/5, Picfive 28/6, Plume Photography 3lt (UV light), Daniel Prudek 20b, Sherri R Camp 17bc, 18b, Racomm 25c, RAStudio 27t (robot), REDPIXEL PL 24/6, Dawid Rojeck 33b, Umberto Shtanzman 35tr (smartphone), Sportpoint 4t, Stockphoto-graf 20t, Syda Prodcutions 25r, Thanapun 28/1, Tinydevil 28/8, TrifonenkoIvan 27t (shop), Chris Turner 36/6, Wavebreakmedia 11b, 12b, Tracy Whiteside 13cr, 15cl, 27cr, 3lbl, John Wollwerth 2lb

All other images © Pearson Education

Every effort has been made to trace the copyright holders and we apologise in advance for any unintentional omissions. We would be pleased to insert the appropriate acknowledgement in any subsequent edition of this publication.

Contents

Sports for All

I will learn about opportunities for everyone to do sport.

 2 **1** **Read, listen, and write. Listen again and check.**

| canoeing   wheelchairs   skiing   gold medal   Paralympics |
| blades   swimming   technology |

Have you heard of the _____? These are Olympic Games for people with special needs or problems. There are a lot of different games in this big event, such as _____ in the Olympic pool, basketball, other water sports like _____, and even _____ in winter.

Athletes taking part in these games usually need help from _____. For example, athletes who play basketball or tennis sit in special _____ to move on the court. For running, athletes use special legs called running _____. These help them run really fast.

This sporting event is very important for the athletes. Winning a _____ in the Paralympics can give people a new interest in life.

2 **Choose a word or phrase from 1. Write.**

a In this sport you travel quickly down a river. _____

b Athletes who have lost a leg can use these to run a race. _____

c This is the first prize in a sports competition. _____

d You do this sport in winter. _____

e This is a competition for athletes with physical problems. _____

f People who can't walk can use this to move. _____

g You get into the water to do this sport. _____

h This uses computers and modern equipment to help athletes.

_____

3 Listen, look, and say.

fearless

carbon fiber

partially blind

4 Match.

1 carbon fiber   a never afraid
2 fearless   b not able to see well
3 partially blind   c a material used to make blades

5 Which sports do you know? Discuss and complete.

ball sports

mountain sports

water sports

_____   _____   _____
_____   _____   _____
_____   _____   _____
_____   _____   _____
_____   _____   _____

6 Which Paralympic sports have you seen? What did you think about them? Tell a partner.

7 ▶ⓥ¹ **Watch. Check (✓) what you hear or see.**

running blades ☐   wheelchair tennis ☐   canoeing ☐
skiing ☐   basketball ☐

8 ▶ⓥ¹ **Watch again. Complete the table.**

Name	Sports	Other information
Rio	_____	His _____ blades help him run really fast.
Andy	_____	He has won a _____ _____ in the Paralympics.
Rob	_____	He says "I am _____."
Charlotte	_____	She helps her friend who is partially _____ .

9 🎧⁴ **Read and complete. Then listen and check.**

| kilometers   radios   wheelchairs   how   direction   instructions |

These are sit skis made for racers who need _____. The ski technology allows winter Paralympians to race at speeds up to 112 _____ an hour.

So _____ do you ski if you are partially blind? This visually-impaired woman uses her friend Charlotte as a guide. Charlotte gives her _____ so that she skis in the right _____ and at the right speed. They communicate using _____.

10 **What would you like to try? Draw lines. Ask and answer with a partner.**

| I love | I'm good at | I don't like | I'm not good at |

| I'm interested in | I'm not interested in |

How about joining the football team?

OK. I love playing football.

11 **Complete the conversation. Then listen and check.**

| playing   interested   great   about   thanks   doing   dancing   joining   How |

Phil: How _____ trying out for the basketball team?

Clara: I don't think so. I'm not good at _____ basketball.

Phil: _____ about joining the canoeing team?

Clara: No, _____. I'm not really _____ in canoeing.

Phil: What do you like _____?

Clara: I enjoy singing. And I like _____ a lot!

Phil: How about _____ the drama club?

Clara: The drama club? Yes! Sounds _____!

THINK BIG

Which sports have you tried?
Which sports would you like to try?

Family Milestones

I will learn about important events in our lives.

 1 Read, listen, and find the photo for each sentence. Write the number.

a It's wonderful to <u>retire</u> after thirty years of hard work!

b When women <u>get married</u> they often wear a white dress.

c When you <u>get a driver's license</u>, you can buy a car.

d I'm just starting university. I'll <u>graduate</u> after three years.

e My little cousin was born a year ago. She's <u>having her first birthday</u> today.

f I <u>got a new job</u>! I start work in a new office tomorrow.

g Our apartment is too small, so we're going to <u>buy a new house</u>.

h My grandparents are <u>celebrating their sixtieth wedding anniversary</u> next week.

2 Look at the underlined events in 1. In which order do they usually happen? Write, then discuss with a partner.

1 _____   5 _____

2 _____   6 _____

3 _____   7 _____

4 _____   8 _____

3 **Listen, look, and say.**

contentment

success

memories

4 **Complete the definitions with words from 3.**

a _____ is when you do something that you wanted to do and worked hard to achieve.

b _____ are the things you remember from the past about a person, place, or experience.

c _____ is a feeling of happiness and being satisfied with what you have.

5 **Think about a recent family celebration. Complete and discuss.**

A family celebration

What was the celebration?

_____

Who was there?

_____

What did you do?

_____

What did you eat?

_____

6 **What milestones does your family celebrate? Tell a partner.**

7 ▶ (v2) **Watch. Check (✓) what you hear or see.**

get a driver's license ☐   celebrate a wedding anniversary ☐

have a first birthday ☐   retire ☐

8 ▶ (v2) **Watch again. Complete the table.**

Name	Celebrating	How they are celebrating
Ollie	_____	with lots of _____
Luke	learning to _____	being happy with his _____
babies in Korea	_____ birthday	a big _____
Patricia and William	60th wedding _____	a small _____
the Queen	_____ years as queen	with _____ of people

9 ◖8◗ **Read and complete. Then listen and check.**

| have   wedding   important   traditions   memories   grow up |

As we grow older, family
_____ and celebrations
are just as _____.
John and Ann are celebrating their
81st _____ anniversary.
They have a lifetime of shared
_____. They watched
their children _____
and get married themselves.

After 81 years, John and Ann are still happily married. What's their secret? Contentment and being happy with what they have.

10 **Read. Ask and answer with a partner.**

Maria / 60 / retire

Ben / 18 / get a driver's license

Manny / 22 / graduate

Jeannie / 5 / start school

Grant / 28 / buy a house

Erica / 31 / get married

When did Maria retire?

Maria retired when she was 60.

11 **Read and complete. Then listen and check.**

I went to university when I _____ 18. I studied hard. _____ I was 21, I graduated. I got my pilot's license and started my first _____ as a pilot when I was 23. A few years _____, I bought a big house near the sea. When I _____ married, I went to live in London with Grandpa. We lived there _____ five years. Your mom had her first birthday there! Then we moved back to the US _____ your mom was two. That was 30 years _____!

THINK BIG

What did you do when you were younger? What are the milestones in your life?

3 Charity Fundraising

Before You Watch

I will learn about raising money to help charities.

🎧 1 Listen, choose, and write. Listen again and check.

| collect | host | do | organize | sell | run | have | get |

Barnham School is raising money for charity.
These are our ideas!

a   The sports coach wants to _____ a marathon.
b   The boys in sixth grade want to _____ a red nose day.
c   The math teacher wants to _____ a used book sale.
d   The principal wants to _____ a sponsored swim.
e   The girls in fifth grade want to have a dress-up day to _____ money.
f   The music teacher wants to _____ a talent show for singers.
g   The football team wants to _____ people to sponsor them to play.
h   The students in seventh grade want to _____ homemade goods.

2 Read and complete with phrases from 1.

a   If you're good at water sports, you can _____.
b   If you like baking cakes, you can _____.
c   If you like old books, you can _____.
d   If you want to make people laugh, you can _____.
e   If you want everyone to wear special clothes, you can _____.
f   If you can run a very long way, you can _____.
g   If students in your class love basketball, you can _____.
h   If your friends like singing and dancing, you can _____.

3 Listen, look, and say.

run in slow motion

make a lemonade stand

hold an eating competition

4 Which of the ideas for raising money in Activity 3 are they talking about?

Anyone can do this – you just have to feel really hungry!

_____

You don't go fast, but you have to be fit.

_____

Choose a hot day. Everyone will be thirsty and you'll raise lots of money!

_____

5 What would you do to raise money for charity? Discuss and complete.

A Charity Fundraiser

Name of event: _____

Where: _____

When: _____

Which charity: _____

What would people have to do: _____

6 Have you ever raised money for charity? What did you do? Who did you raise money for? Tell a partner.

7 **Watch. Check (✓) what you hear or see.**

organize a red nose day ☐

host a talent show ☐

do a sponsored swim ☐

sell homemade goods ☐

run a marathon ☐

hold an eating competition ☐

8 **Watch again. Complete the table.**

Fundraiser	What do people do?	What do they raise money for?
_____ Nose Day	wear a funny nose	to help people in poor _____
Marathon run in _____	_____ very slowly	to find ways to make _____ people better
Eating _____	eat lots of meatballs	to help people hurt in an earthquake in _____

9 **Read and complete. Then listen and check.**

| raise   posters   event   homemade   lemonade   charity |

Not every _____ needs to be so grand to help charity. Selling _____ goods is an enjoyable and creative way to _____ money for charity. Delicious _____, made by some schoolgirls, is selling well to passers-by. The girls give all the money they make to _____. They have even made _____ to advertise their stall.

10 **How could you raise money? Draw lines. Ask and answer with a partner.**

for our club   for our class trip   for our team   for the hospital   for our school

  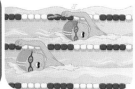  

How could we raise money for our club?

We could run a marathon.

11 **Complete the conversation. Then listen and check.**

Jaime: _____ could we raise money for the soccer club?

Sophie: We could do a _____ swim.

Jaime: I'm not into swimming. What else could we _____?

Sophie: Ummm … We _____ have a cake sale.

Jaime: That's a great idea! I love baking. How _____ could we sell the cakes for?

Sophie: One dollar each.

Jaime: OK. I _____ going to make lots of cakes. We're _____ to raise lots of money!

Sophie: How _____ we going to tell people about the sale?

Jaime: You're going _____ make posters!

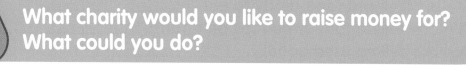

THINK BIG **What charity would you like to raise money for? What could you do?**

Let's Go Shopping

I will learn about shopping in different places.

1 **Read and listen. Where would you buy old things?**

In the past, people bought the things they needed at small shops near their house. You got bread in one shop and fruit in another. Now, people buy most of their food in a <u>supermarket</u> and their clothes in a big <u>department store</u>. But a small <u>convenience store</u> still sells basic things like milk and newspapers.

You can shop outdoors too. The fruit and vegetables at a <u>farmers' market</u> are very fresh! Eating outside at a <u>street food stall</u> is cheaper than going to a restaurant.

If you want to buy old things cheaply, you can go to a <u>flea market</u>. An <u>auction</u> is more expensive. At an auction, everyone says what they want to pay for an item and the person who offers the most money gets it!

At home, we can use our computers to shop <u>online</u>. But a shopping <u>mall</u> is a great place to meet your friends – there are lots of shops and cafés there!

2 **Read and write the correct store from 1.**

   a Somewhere you can buy things using a computer or tablet. _____

   b A large store with different areas. _____

   c A small store that is open until late at night. _____

   d A large building with many stores inside. _____

   e Somewhere you buy things by offering more money than other people. _____

   f A large store that sells food and things for the house. _____

   g Stalls which sell food ready to eat. _____

   h A place selling food produced on a farm. _____

   i A place selling used goods. _____

3 **Listen, look, and say.**

bargain

produce

vintage

profit

4 **Complete the sentences with words from 3.**

a I don't have much money so I like to look for a _____.

b If you want something old and unusual, go to the flea market. You'll find many _____ treasures there!

c If you buy something for $10 and sell it for $20, you have made a _____.

d I like farmers' markets because they sell local _____, like fruit and vegetables.

5 **Where do you like to go shopping? Complete and discuss.**

indoors

outdoors

online

_____ _____ _____

_____ _____ _____

6 **What different shopping places have you been to? What did you buy? Tell a partner.**

7 **Watch. Number the words and phrases in the order you hear or see them.**

mall ☐   street food market ☐

department store ☐   supermarket ☐

auction ☐   farmers' market ☐

8 **Watch again. Circle to complete the sentences.**

a The street food in Lebanon is **awful / delicious**.

b People make the street food **in a big store / on the street**.

c Local people **eat / don't eat** street food.

d Shopping at a supermarket is **too boring / interesting**.

e The produce in vegetable stalls **is locally grown / comes from far away**.

f At a flea market you can try to get a bargain by offering **more / less** money.

g A flea market sells clothes you **can / can't** find in a mall.

h Dealers buy things at auctions, then sell them for **more / less** money to make a profit.

9 **Read and complete the poem. Then listen and check.**

markets	phone	prices	store	fun	buy

Stay out of the mall if you want
some good _____.
Weekend _____ offer
excitement for everyone.
A great place to hang out
And _____ stuff with friends.
Haggle down _____
until the day ends.
Browse T-shirts and gadgets,
_____ cases galore,
And clothes that aren't copied in a
shopping mall _____.

10 Compare the different places to shop with a partner.

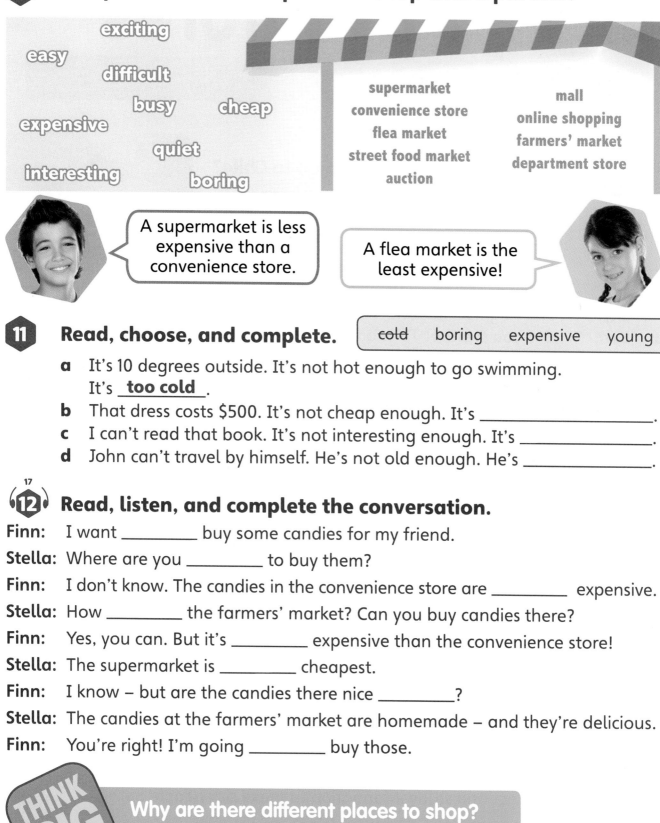

exciting
easy
difficult
busy   cheap
expensive
quiet
interesting   boring

supermarket
convenience store
flea market
street food market
auction

mall
online shopping
farmers' market
department store

A supermarket is less expensive than a convenience store.

A flea market is the least expensive!

11 Read, choose, and complete.

~~cold~~   boring   expensive   young

a   It's 10 degrees outside. It's not hot enough to go swimming.
    It's __too cold__ .
b   That dress costs $500. It's not cheap enough. It's _____.
c   I can't read that book. It's not interesting enough. It's _____.
d   John can't travel by himself. He's not old enough. He's _____.

17
12 Read, listen, and complete the conversation.

Finn: I want _____ buy some candies for my friend.

Stella: Where are you _____ to buy them?

Finn: I don't know. The candies in the convenience store are _____ expensive.

Stella: How _____ the farmers' market? Can you buy candies there?

Finn: Yes, you can. But it's _____ expensive than the convenience store!

Stella: The supermarket is _____ cheapest.

Finn: I know – but are the candies there nice _____?

Stella: The candies at the farmers' market are homemade – and they're delicious.

Finn: You're right! I'm going _____ buy those.

THINK BIG   Why are there different places to shop?
Why do people prefer different places?

5 Vacation Adventures

Before You Watch

I will learn about unusual vacation places.

1 18 🎧 **Read and listen. Who wants to go to Chile?**

a Lily: We're going to Paris this year. Isn't that great? We'll see lots of interesting places.

Tom: Oh, no! Not more <u>sightseeing</u>! I really want to go to the beach and learn <u>snorkeling</u>. Think of seeing all those fish!

Lily: Ah – sightseeing underwater!

b Ben: Did you see that TV program about <u>medical research</u>, Ana?

Ana: You mean the one where they climbed <u>Mount Everest</u>? Yes, I did. Imagine climbing a mountain to do research!

c Julie: My brother's going to <u>the Arctic</u>. He's going to visit the North Pole!

Phil: Is he traveling on an <u>icebreaker</u>? A big ship like that is the safest way to travel through icy waters.

d Dad: Let's go to an <u>exotic country</u> this year!

Mom: Yes – somewhere really different would be great. What about Chile? We could go to the Atacama Desert – and you can go down a <u>silver mine</u> and find out how they get the metal out of the earth.

2 **Choose a word or phrase from 1. Write.**

a A large boat you need in very icy water. _____

b A place underground where you can dig for metal. _____

c A very snowy place – the North Pole is there. _____

d When you look at interesting buildings and places on vacation. _____

e An interesting and unusual place. _____

f The highest mountain in the world. _____

g When you collect and study information to make sick people better.

_____

h An activity where you swim with your face underwater. _____

3 Listen, look, and say.

tourist

ancient monument

dynamite

4 Read the definitions and write the words from 3.

a This is used to cause an explosion. The explosion gets metal out of the ground.

_____

b This is someone who visits a place on vacation.

_____

c This is a building or other special feature of a place that people like to visit. It's very old.

_____

5 Write all the things you like to do on vacation. Then discuss with your partner.

Things to do on vacation

_____

_____

_____

_____

_____

_____

_____

6 What is the most exciting vacation you have been on? Tell a partner.

7 ▶ᵥ₅ **Watch. Number in the order you hear or see them.**

sightseeing ☐   medical research ☐
dynamite ☐   snorkeling ☐
the Arctic ☐   an icebreaker ☐
tourists ☐

8 ▶ᵥ₅ **Watch again. Complete the table.**

Place	Vacation activity
Qatar	relaxing in a _____
the Maldives	_____
Rome	_____
the Arctic	taking _____ of polar bears
Bolivia	exploring the silver _____
Nepal	doing medical _____

9 ₍₂₀₎ **Read and complete. Then listen and check.**

| very | boat | Finland | swimming | vacation |

A few hundred miles away, in _____, these tourists are on a special _____ built for _____ cold waters: an icebreaker. A surprising number of people choose to go on this freezing _____.

The captain says, "We have approximately ten thousand tourists per year."

The visitors are now ready to go _____ in the icy waters.

10 **Read and write. Then ask and answer with a partner.**

a

Susie – snorkel – she – see a whale

When Susie was snorkeling, she saw a whale.

b

Ryan – visit an exotic country – he – meet a tiger

_____

c

Zander – visit ancient monuments in Rome – he – get lost

_____

d

Zoe – travel on an icebreaker – she – take this photo

_____

e

Katie – climb Mount Everest – she – hurt her leg

_____

What was Susie doing when she saw a whale?

She was snorkeling when she saw a whale.

 21

11 **Complete the conversation. Then listen and check.**

Manu: Have you heard? Anna is in the hospital! She hurt her arm.

Aisha: Oh, no! _____ was she doing when she got hurt?

Manu: She _____ biking with her family yesterday _____ it started to rain.

Aisha: What happened?

Manu: She fell off _____ she was going down a hill.

Aisha: _____ she going too fast when she fell off?

Manu: Yes, she _____.

THINK BIG

Imagine the most exciting vacation you can. What happened?

6 Robot World

I will learn about robots and what they can do.

1 **Match the underlined words to the photos. Write the number.**

a With a <u>digital camera</u>, photographers can _____ thousands of photos and erase the ones they don't like. ☐

b A <u>tablet</u> is much lighter than a laptop so it's easier to _____. ☐

c I'd love to have a <u>robot</u> in the house to _____ all the housework! ☐

d People create <u>avatars</u> when they _____ interactive video games. ☐

e I've got a new <u>computer</u> to _____ my work quicker and easier. ☐

f I'll have to get a new <u>speaker</u> for my CD player because I can't _____ the music. ☐

g Some people _____ a mouse with their screen, but others prefer a <u>touchscreen</u>. ☐

h You can hear me through the headphones and _____ to me using the <u>microphone</u>. ☐

2 **22** **Read and complete the sentences in 1. Then listen and check.**

| play | use | carry | hear | make | take | do | speak |

3 **Read and write the correct technology word from 1.**

a I think this _____ is broken. When I tap it like this, nothing happens.

b The best way to take photos is with a _____.

c If you want to make a recording, speak into the _____.

d The music is really loud! These are great _____.

e Scientists often use _____ to do work that is too dangerous for people.

f My uncle doesn't like _____. He prefers to write everything by hand.

g Have you chosen your _____ for the game?

h My mom's laptop was too heavy to carry around, so she bought a _____.

23

4 **Listen, look, and say.**

crew    receptionist    social contact

5 **Complete the sentences with words from 4.**

a When you are ill and in bed, you miss the _____ with your friends.

b All the members of the _____ had different jobs to do.

c When we arrived at the hospital, the _____ told us where to wait.

6 **What would you like a robot to do for you? Why? Complete and discuss.**

What kind of robot? _____

Task: _____

Reason: _____

7 **What electronic devices do you use? What do you use them for? Tell a partner.**

8 ▶(v6) **Watch. Number the items in the order you hear or see them.**

speakers ☐   touchscreen ☐

tablet ☐   microphone ☐

camera ☐   avatar ☐

9 ▶(v6) **Watch again. Check (✓) the sentences which are correct.**

a   The little robots are part of an airplane crew. ☐
b   A robot in the USA teaches children at school. ☐
c   Robots can help sick children have less social contact. ☐
d   The avatar does the student's homework. ☐
e   Students can use their phones to control what the avatar does. ☐
f   The avatar can take photos. ☐
g   Pepper is a robot receptionist in Norway. ☐
h   Pepper helps children at the hospital. ☐

10 (24) **Read and complete. Then listen and check.**

desk	avatar	speaks	ears	tablet	microphones

In Norway, there is a robot that kids use in school. One woman describes the robot this way: "This is an _____, so an extension of yourself. So it sits at the child's _____ in the classroom and the child uses a _____ or a phone to start it, control its movements with touch, and talk through it. So it's their eyes and their _____ and their voice. So it has speakers and _____ and cameras, and when the child _____ at home or in the hospital to his iPad it just comes out through this one, so it's really a super, super fancy phone."

11 **Think and choose. Ask and answer with a partner.**

yes / no   yes / no   yes / no   yes / no   yes / no

Do you think we'll have stores 100 years from now?

No, we won't. We'll buy everything online.

12 **Complete the conversation. Then listen and check.**

Paulo: Do you think _____ have tablets 100 years from now?

Jen: No, we _____.

Paulo: How _____ we send messages?

Jen: Everyone will have a smartwatch. They _____ use that to send messages. _____ you think we'll have schools 100 years from now?

Paulo: _____, we will. But no one will _____ to school. We'll all have avatars in a virtual classroom.

THINK BIG

What do you think will be different in the future? How?

7 Great Invention

Before You Watch

I will learn about a recent invention.

1 Read and listen. Then match the underlined words to the photos.

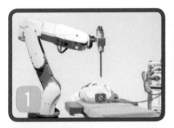

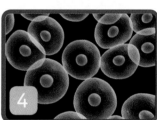

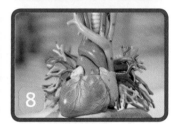

a Today we are going to learn about the tiny <u>cells</u> which make up our bodies. Tomorrow, we are going to study a very special organ: the human <u>heart</u>.

b Last night, I saw a really informative TV program. It was about how some <u>3D printers</u> use <u>UV light</u> to make interesting things. It was really good!

c Do you want to listen to your music without anyone else hearing? Use a <u>headset</u>. Choose one made of <u>plastic</u> – it's light and it doesn't break.

d Our cakes are always perfect. That's because we use <u>robotic arms</u> to mix the <u>ingredients</u>!

2 Read and write the correct word or phrase from 1.

a The ocean is so full of _____ that fish are dying in many places.

b _____ are so small you need a microscope to see them.

c One use of _____ is to make things very clean.

d They use a _____ to make cars in this factory.

e Doctors say that too much salt is bad for your _____.

f I need to buy a _____ so that I can watch films when my brother is asleep.

g A _____ can make all kinds of objects.

h The ice-creams in that shop are delicious! They only use fresh _____.

3 Listen, look, and say.

invention

patterns

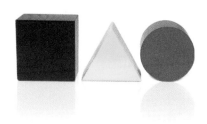
shapes

4 Complete the sentences with words from 3.

a A square, a circle, and a rectangle are all types of _____.

b _____ are shapes, colors, or lines that repeat regularly.

c An _____ is a useful machine or tool that someone has thought of for the first time.

5 What recent inventions do you have at home? Where are they? Complete and discuss.

Invention	Use	Room
Internet TV	stream movies & TV	living room

6 What do you think has been the greatest invention? Why? Tell a partner.

7 ▶v7 **Watch. Number the items in the order you hear or see them.**

ingredients ☐ 3D printer ☐ plastic ☐

robotic arms ☐ UV light ☐ human cells ☐

8 ▶v7 **Watch again. Circle to complete the sentences.**

a The 3D printers are used to make **food / books**.
b They can print **just one shape / lots of shapes**.
c The 3D printers can print objects using **wood / plastic**.
d **Ink / UV light** is used in the 3D printing process.
e Easton Lachappelle has made **robotic arms / human hair** using a 3D printer.
f His models are **cheap / expensive**.
g A headset is used to **design / move** the arm.
h In the future, we will use 3D printers to **travel to other planets / help sick people**.

9 28 **Read and complete. Then listen and check.**

| injured | body | 3D printers | human cells | technology | hearts |

_____ are getting very sophisticated. They can even make artificial skin for people who have been _____.

This machine is designed to use _____. It's not ready yet, but scientists are developing this printer to be able to create new _____ or kidneys.

A scientist says about 3D printing that "One of the future applications of this _____ is that you would be able to then harvest your own healthy cells from anywhere in your _____ and reprogram those to be the organ specifically that you want to create."

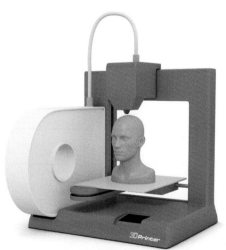

10 **Match. Then ask and answer with a partner.**

 robotic arm

 plastic

 headset

 UV light

 3D printer

 print toys

 control electronic devices

 make bags

 clean water

 make cars

What is a robotic arm used for?

It's used for making cars.

11 **Complete the conversation. Then listen and check.**

Harry: What's this used _____?

Nina: It's a 3D printer. It's used _____ create 3D objects.

Harry: Wow! _____ kind of things?

Nina: Fun things like musical instruments, cell phone cases, toys, cups, shoes ... And really useful things _____ robotic arms.

Harry: What _____ robotic arms used for?

Nina: They're _____ for building things like cars and telescopes.

 **THINK BIG**

Imagine you've got a 3D printer. What do you make with it? Why?

8 Food Miles

Before You Watch

I will learn about the distance food travels.

 1 **Read and listen. Why does Bill worry about bringing food from far away?**

Interviewer: Today our guest speaker is Bill Jackson. Bill runs an <u>urban farm</u> – that's a farm in the middle of the city! It's a <u>community farm</u>, so everyone in his neighborhood works there. Bill, tell us why you decided to start the farm.

Bill: I've always been interested in <u>agriculture</u>. I like growing things. I also worry about using cars and planes to bring food from far away. It's bad for the environment and causes <u>climate change</u>.

Interviewer: So you decided to cut down on <u>food miles</u> by growing lots of fruit and vegetables here. Is that right?

Bill: Yes, that's the idea. We produce <u>organic food</u> because it's healthier than food grown using chemicals. Our fruit and vegetables are full of <u>nutrients</u>. We only keep them in our <u>warehouse</u> for a few days. Then we deliver them to people who live in the town. That way, they're fresh and healthy, and they don't travel far.

Interviewer: Thank you for talking to us today, Bill. Good luck with the farm!

2 **Read and complete with the correct underlined word or phrase from 1.**

a I live in the city, but I grow vegetables in my yard. I have my own _____!

b The company stores all their goods in a _____.

c He is studying _____ at university because he wants to be a farmer.

d This is very healthy food. It has lots of different _____.

e We use too much fuel. This causes _____ and other problems for the environment.

f Everyone around here wanted to grow fresh food. We started a _____.

g I love pineapples, but they come from very far away. That's a lot of _____!

h I buy _____ because it's healthier than food grown using chemicals.

31
3 Listen, look, and say.

| continent | cocoa beans | coffee beans | exporting |

4 Read the definitions and write the words from 3.

a Chocolate is made from these. _____

b A place like Europe, Africa, or Antarctica. _____

c This is the business of selling and sending goods to other countries.

_____

d A hot drink is made from these. It tastes slightly bitter.

_____

5 What did you eat yesterday? Where did it come from? Complete and discuss.

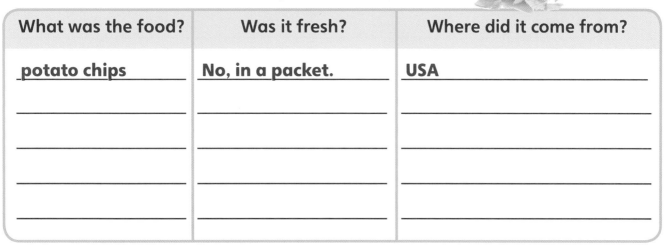

What was the food?	Was it fresh?	Where did it come from?
potato chips	No, in a packet.	USA

6 Which do you think is the most important? Read and number in order. Then discuss with a partner.

Food that is …

☐ cheap ☐ delicious ☐ local ☐ healthy ☐ quick to prepare

7 ▶⑧ **Watch. Number the items in the order you hear or see them.**

climate change ☐   nutrients ☐   food miles ☐
warehouses ☐   agriculture ☐   community farm ☐

8 ▶⑧ **Watch again. Check (✓) the sentences which are correct.**

a Coffee is enjoyed in lots of different countries. ☐
b Bananas are grown locally in most countries. ☐
c If a plane brings food from far away, this uses a lot of fuel. ☐
d It is good for the planet if we burn lots of fuel. ☐
e Food miles tell us how far food travels before we eat it. ☐
f Food is fresher if it doesn't have to travel far. ☐
g Growing fresh organic fruit and vegetables is very easy. ☐
h Vertical agriculture uses a lot of water. ☐
i Mushrooms grow well in cold, dark, wet places. ☐

9 🎧 ³² **Read and complete. Then listen and check.**

| less   agriculture   near   made   grow   nutrients |

In this New Jersey-based company, in the USA, they are taking a scientific approach and have developed a method for what they call "vertical _____". It allows them to _____ food indoors, making the most of the available space.

The food is grown on pieces of reusable cloth _____ out of recycled water bottles, and needs _____ water, fewer _____, and zero pesticides. The result is organic produce grown very _____ the people who will get to eat it.

ORGANIC FARM

After You Watch

10 **Look and write. Then ask and answer with a partner.**

a <u>**The most colorful flowers are sold in the Netherlands.**</u>
(sell)

b Very tasty avocados _____.
(grow)

c The most exciting phones _____.
(design)

d The most delicious ice-cream _____.
(produce)

e The softest cotton _____.
(export by)

What is sold in the Netherlands?

The most colorful flowers are sold in the Netherlands.

11 **Complete the conversation. Then listen and check.**

33

Maria: Do you know where that banana was grown?

Jackie: Ummm … no.

Maria: Bananas are _____ in countries very far away. They are packed carefully, then they _____ sent on planes all over the world. That banana has done a lot of food _____.

Jackie: Oh. Is that bad?

Maria: It uses a lot of fuel – and that makes _____ change worse.

Jackie: What should I do?

Maria: Buy food that _____ produced locally. Forget bananas! Try local organic apples. They're delicious!

Jackie: Where can I buy them?

Maria: They are _____ at the farmers' market.

What food do you eat that comes from far away? Where is it grown? How far does it travel?

Unit 8   35

q Extreme Sports

I will learn about dangerous and exciting sports.

1 Read and listen. Then match the underlined words to the photos.

a If you are afraid of high places, don't go <u>mountain climbing</u> or <u>skydiving</u>.

b For great <u>surfing</u>, you need big waves. Fast rivers are good for <u>white water rafting</u>.

c When you go <u>sandboarding</u>, you travel fast downhill on a board. <u>Zorbing</u> is even more exciting – you go downhill inside a big ball!

d You need a special type of bike to go <u>mountain biking</u>.

e <u>Pole climbing</u> is popular. People compete to get to the top first.

2 Read and write the correct extreme sport from 1.

a My brother loves _____ outside the city. He rides his bike every weekend.

b When I went _____, I felt frightened before I jumped out of the plane.

c Judy fell into the river when she went _____!

d This is a popular beach for _____ because the waves are so big.

e When we went _____ down the hill, I crashed and my board broke.

f A lot of people go _____ in the Himalayas.

g Our sports teacher organized a _____ competition. I got to the top last!

h When Jo went _____, the ball went very quickly down the hill.

🎧 35

3 Listen, look, and say.

volcano

avalanche

adrenaline rush

4 Complete the sentences with words from 3.

a When you do extreme sports, you get a feeling of great excitement. This is called an _____.

b Mountain climbers have to be very careful not to get caught in an _____.

c When a _____ is active, it could erupt. Then it is a very dangerous place to be.

5 What extreme things would you like to try? Complete and discuss.

Extreme activities	Extreme food	Extreme theme park attractions
snowboarding	very hot chilies	rollercoaster

6 Which extreme sports do you find the most exciting? List them in order, from most exciting to most boring.

most exciting ➤ most boring

7 ▶(v9) **Watch. Number the extreme sports in the order you hear or see them. Which sports aren't mentioned?**

pole climbing ☐   skydiving ☐   mountain climbing ☐

surfing ☐   sandboarding ☐

8 ▶(v9) **Watch again. Circle to complete the sentences.**

a   The sand surfers go sandboarding **at the beach / on a volcano**.

b   The sand surfers travel at up to **eighteen / eighty** kilometers an hour.

c   You feel an adrenaline rush when you are **scared or excited / tired or bored**.

d   Adrenaline **helps you breathe / gives you energy**.

e   In an avalanche, the snow **melts / falls down the mountain**.

f   Crossing the cracks in the ice is **dangerous / tiring**.

g   The weather on the mountain is **good / bad**.

h   It is important to **stop / keep going** if there is real danger.

9 (36)🎧 **Read and complete. Then listen and check.**

| extreme | good | enjoy | win | dangerous | energy |

Many people like to push themselves to the limit, which is why _____ sports are so popular. It seems strange that people will choose to do things that look _____, but they do. So let's take a look at some extreme sports and try to find out why people _____ them.

One extreme sport is pole climbing. One man who does this sport says, "I love it. I just love the burst of _____ and the adrenaline that you get just from charging up the pole."

The adrenaline rush puts this racer's muscles into action and helps him _____ the race. The extra energy also makes him feel _____.

10 **Write five more sports for each category. Then choose, and ask and answer with a partner.**

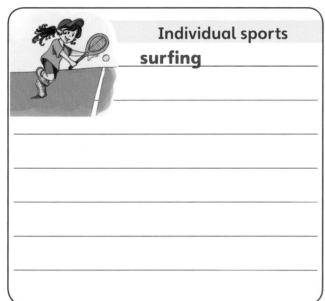

Individual sports

surfing _____

_____

_____

_____

_____

_____

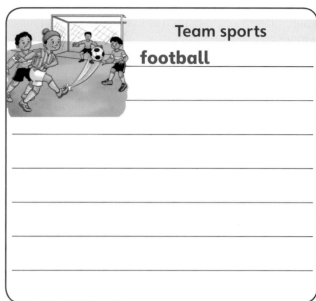

Team sports

football _____

_____

_____

_____

_____

_____

Would you rather go surfing or play football?

I'd rather play football. What about you?

37

11 **Complete the conversation. Then listen and check.**

Nadia: Have you _____ been sandboarding?

Rory: _____, I haven't. Have you?

Nadia: Yes, I _____. But it was too fast! I didn't really like it.

Rory: What kind of sports _____ you like?

Nadia: I love doing water sports. I _____ enjoy swimming.

Rory: _____ you rather try white water rafting or surfing?

Nadia: I'd _____ try surfing. It looks fun!

THINK BIG

Why do some people like to do dangerous sports? How do they choose which sport to do?

Word List

① Sports for All

blades
canoeing
gold medal
Paralympics
skiing
swimming
technology
wheelchairs
carbon fiber
fearless
partially blind

② Family Milestones

buy a new house
celebrate a wedding anniversary
get a driver's license
get a job
get married
graduate
have a first birthday
retire
contentment
memories
success

③ Charity Fundraising

collect money
do a sponsored swim
get people to sponsor you
have a dress-up day
have a used book sale
host a talent show
organize a red nose day
run a marathon
sell homemade goods
hold an eating competition
make a lemonade stand
run in slow motion

④ Let's Go Shopping

auction
convenience store
department store
farmers' market
flea market
mall
street food stall
supermarket
indoors
online
outdoors
bargain
produce
profit
vintage

⑤ Vacation Adventures

the Arctic
exotic country
icebreaker
medical research
Mount Everest
sightseeing
silver mine
snorkeling
ancient monument
dynamite
tourist

⑥ Robot World

avatar
computer
digital camera
microphone
robot
speaker
tablet
touchscreen
crew
receptionist
social contact

⑦ Great Invention

3D printer
cells
headset
heart
ingredients
plastic
robotic arm
UV light
invention
patterns
shapes

⑧ Food Miles

agriculture
climate change
community farm
food miles
nutrients
organic food
urban farm
warehouse
continent
cocoa beans
coffee beans
exporting

⑨ Extreme Sports

mountain biking
mountain climbing
pole climbing
sandboarding
skydiving
surfing
white water rafting
zorbing
adrenaline rush
avalanche
volcano